Wolf Moon

a book of hours

Cover, *Le Loup* by Georges Liautaud
from the Albert Grokoest collection
with gratitude

photograph by Larry Kefferstan

Book design by Judith Fletcher

First Printing, April 1974
Second Printing, October 1974

ALICE JAMES BOOKS
138 Mount Auburn Street
Cambridge, Massachusetts 02138

Note

While the men were on the moon, I looked at it. It not only appeared to be still there, it appeared to be the same moon of antiquity and myth. Also the moon of interplay that humps the water up from the oceans, that causes the tonsillectomies to hemorrhage, that fills the maternity wards when *it* fills.

It seemed to be still affecting to lunatics and lovers. I was touched by this mystery: I still think of it as mine.

for Laurence Dick and John Pedrick
who let me be

Acknowledgements are due to the following publications in whose pages some of these poems first appeared: *Encounter,* for "The Match Girl"; *The Little Magazine,* for "Guerrilla Attack: New Hampshire," "Horn," "The Stag at Eve" and "Sturgeon Moon"; *LET'S EAT THE CHILDREN, An Anthology,* Cambridge Street Artists Cooperative, 1972, for "Buck and Wing: Wooden Toys" and "Hot Moon."

Wolf Moon

Jean Pedrick

Contents

Quince: But there is two hard things; that is to bring the moon-light into a chamber: for you know, Pyramus and Thisby meet by moon-light.

Snug: Doth the moon shine, that night we play our play?

Bottom: A calendar, a calendar! look in the almanac; find out moon-shine. . .

— *Midsummer-night's Dream*

The moon has vanished.*

— Andrei Voznesensky
Look Out for Your Faces

* In Russian this is a palindrome,
A luna kanula.

Wolf Moon

The year has fangs even in infancy, and sits
gaunt, up-thrusted from its bony haunches,
sits in a ring of mist (who are
the white things? what's out there?)
moves hardly perceived — all seem to be
still seated and move toward the fire.

We ring around our fire, rosy as apples.
Our juices, warmed, release our hot strange spices
one to another as though on winds between islands.

Werewolf

I have watched them look up into news
camera lenses, the deranged murderers.
With a meek gaze like soft-mouth berry
eating animals; with hands uneasy at seams, at
junctures where pockets came in other jackets,
at nothings, tatting the air —

Murder dreams are separate. Somebody else
has dreamed them. *He* likes sun.
Dust bouncing in it, the gesture
of kindness it lays on his arms.
(He likes some other things, sibilant
lady clothes, perhaps tall mocha cakes —
it seldom is one's birthday.) There are things
of course, he can't stand, but never knows
when those will happen, or remembers too late.

Rage comes down like scarlet water.
There is no witness in him. The sun
itches the tracks of brambles on his arms.
It wasn't brambles, it was fingernails
of girls. He hides or incinerates objects.
Something like memory tells him what to do.
His eyes peep out like martyrs. Scourge the world.

The Match Girl

(Prague)

Nearby the Opera in the snow
where minks and stoats and fitches go
big as behemoths, to and fro,

the little match girl lights her hair.
The dead quicken. The quick stare.

Later Salomé serves her thing —
Cordon Bleu of the Horseshoe ring —
triumph *au jus* all glistering

and yet she is upstaged. They go
haunted by embers in the snow.

Guerrilla Attack: New Hampshire

"Shoot anything that moves."
— *verbal order in a Vietnam village*

The house was small, double a chicken-coop
but smaller than "Splt lvl, 5rm, frplce, cozy
new rnch w. pictr windw." Somewhere between,
a residence for someone somewhere between.
Half shingle, half tarpaper, half the shingles
dipped in a phloxy, chalking pink (Barn Red
on the paint cans) half still the nude
wet straw color of old, bleached hair
before shampoo — it gathered here and there
a run of resin like a tear.
                    Marty was ironing.
Roy was reading the L. L. Bean. Edie was rapt,
putting, by squirt-bottle, well-water weewee back
in her concave, whistling Christmas doll. "Royden,
let out the dog," the woman said. It pranced,
its claws like tap shoes on the vinyl floor,
window to door to woodshed door, and snuffled
along the weather-strips and thresholds; gulped
hints of disaster into butterfly lungs, flopped,
tail-wagged, fell down in a senile doze,
growled in its sleep, started and pranced again.
"Hey, Roy," she said.
                    "I hear you — put the dog out."

He opened the door on the moon-struck, half-made yard,
its soft, snow-tufted hill of loam, its fairy ring
of thaw and freeze and thaw around the cess-pool.

Hit on the lope by a silenced shot, the dog
crimped up and died half-way across the yard
before Roy had the door to. He took down the gun
that plugged at pheasant sometimes in the fall
but didn't like to hold steady, sighting deer.
"I think there's something funny going on," he said,
and went out sniffing the open arc of danger.

Marty uprooted the iron cord from the socket.
Her head recoiled into her snow-flake sweater.
She moved as though the devil pulled her by the tits,
ran out. And left the mothering little girl —
Edythe Catherine Phaneuf, four years, eight months —
clamped to her doll in the blast of the gaping door.

Snow Moon

There is a stretch of prairie in the mind,
one little frontier more. Our city hulks
around us in a creaking ring; it is
a caravan stopped; the wheeling chimneys
whinny; snow drives like a dust storm
into all the rifts between our needs. `

I say to the fire: *Make me warm.*
You say to the nurse with the pills:
What good will they do?

All prairie ripples between, a virgin field
where not so much as a rabbit's foot kicks up
track from a life. Deserted silences
swallow our several echoes — hunger, anger

Earthworm

Earthworms, a gentleman told me gravely
mate oddly, or oddly to us. Loosing a band
of membrane in turn, and by sweet ritual
each worming its way into the other,
they lie at last (and at length) all intimate
rolled in a single winding-sheet of self
and other self.

                (He was a naturalist born
who also discoursed on the mating octopi
with all those lucky arms who wrap and hold,
one sphere sufficient unto itself for days.)

But what goes on in there between the earthworms
lain like stopped trains must need to burst
its skin; to claw; to flail trackless
reaching or legging it; must need switches —
hope and collision and letting go.

Worm Moon

We live, if underground. A happy choice
it isn't, but we live. Hurrying hard heels
(sociologist ladies late for meetings)
click on our labyrinths. Dropping a dandruff
of addenda — irrelevant recent observations
on quiet violets caught by snow, growing up
in Samoa in, for example, Middlesex suburbs —
novelists, too, some poets, and half the doctors
run, clacking like that: ran us to ground.

Lightless we have illumined one another, true
intent like a torch in a cap that searches
brother for brother in bituminous drifts.
We gleam with lustre of our work; we are
the worm moon's only children, relegates of darkness. . .

Tunnel traversed with you was more than tunnel.
We broke the rind of the sun for more than sun.

Inchworm

Measure me for need.
The wry and stinging inner cheek
extorts the white-milk honey
from my mother. Fear —
contraction — huddles within
the long looped comfort
of her arms, her nest.

Tailor me for joy.
Succulence, pierced, explodes
juice like a ginger bubble
up my throat; boy-stridency
calls to my dusks *Ring-leave-O*.
Fit me to the lift of kites.
Frill me for waltzes.

Fashion me for lust.
For entrechats of meeting in
the Bois. Clothe me in all
the shatter of my colours
loosed by light, band me
in shackles as I let him go,
style me to sleeve relief.

For work, equip me.
Shape hollow, tension, carefulness
of hand to fit good tools.
Test willow in the bone.
Measure my hours, my ardor
while the ingots whiten,
while the silk-looms sing.

Inchworm, fit me for grace
an apple face, the smile that welcomes-home —
blossom, liquor and seed intact (recalled)
and the whole held in privilege
like drops fermented in the whited grass
hard by the original tree.

Vampire

Is there no middle earth?

He drinks the early spade-leaf
violets from my blood
then bluets, flags, whole season's
orders of flowers, all my blue
field of courage. . .

I know there are book ways
to slake the thirst. To meet
at noon, or in mirrors,
bless him, peg his damned heart.
Is there no middle way?

Is there no bosky glade
in amiable woods,
one corner of the glen
between revenge and pain
where dark angels can rise
lucky as Christ again,
Abel learn bark and berries
from a loving Cain?

He sucks me dry
as the stiff wings, cramped claws
of a dead flittermouse.
And yet he drinks me
for a lively need

groping for middle earth.

Crucifixus

Heightened perception heightens pain.
There are fires in the red flowers
that burn the retina. Look away
into the cone's after-garden, the garden
of the dead where we need God
like a dead man a leech,
to fix and flatten on us
and draw out the death.

Shall I blow wild and weightless
as a witch in the wind all
attitudes akimbo, or go down to cover,
hide in cavernous grief; the tenebrae
of adorations snuffed out one by one
while dishpan clangors of the matin-vesper
bells at St. Margarets in the Square
divide the days for ladies
lucky in love who bake the host
Christ after Christ in rows on cookie sheets,
round as buttons and white as paper?

I love, I sense, I suffer.
They love, they pray and bake, have grace.
And yet your face only illumined His.

Crucifixus etiam pro nobis
et sepultus est. . .
to teach us that our mouth is dust,
our mouthful, darkness.

The Tomb

He is inside
but can and must
and will come out.
We will design
him ways, we will
trump the eye: Black,
we will say, a hole;
then blacker, that hole
stoppered; and there begin.

As though delineated from within,
arch, dome, sky-door open
like stretched skin. Salvation
pipping — monstrously strong
because no help — comes forth
from his chamber wearing spiked down
like a drenched crown of thorns.

Egg

Pysanka, the Ukrainian art of inscribing designs on Easter eggs, carries with it the belief that while this rite is continued, the world will continue. Each egg displaces, the old folk say, an ovum of evil waiting to hatch on the world.

The egg lightens
with the years
like the Lord's burdens.
The content powders.

Outside, finely drawn
with a brass stylus
made on Holy Monday
(the major thing,
with bells and horns,
that brass is for)
painted through the pen's cone
by running bees-wax
(wax the third labor of bees)

Dipped after waxing
in the yellow dye,
then brass and wax again,
then dipped in deeper dye:
again, and each tint deeper
through blood-like red,
purple, black, black. . .

The designs unfurl in the genes.
Boy learns from man,
who learned from the old man,
back to the oldest man
with a basket of eggs
in memory (Simon called Peter,
a farm-man from the Ukraine.)

Pink Moon

There is a core of fire in earth things.
Fire in green hyacinths cracks their skulls
on the crust of winter; fire in fiddleheads
stands them in ice like invalids choosing:
Shall we live or die? Fire pushes up
small beasts from hibernation — sleepers awake
with feet in smouldering bogs of dreams.

Carnation moon, this fire of earth reflected,
floats vulnerable as a beamish child.
We grasp what death is cooling like the earth
the instant that we know (waked from the drowse,
disfocus, desperation of infancy)
that we are living. Shadows of our blood
drift like cherry petals across the moon.

Fleur-de-Lis

The King of France
With twenty-thousand men
Marched up the hill
And then marched down again.

A good botanical drawing
pares life along the vertical,
discovers, *en bas,* in the loam,
the cellars of the well-provisioned home,
systems of life support, the privy sources.

In the fenestered stem, regard,
the cellular carefulness, the reed within
tensed for the pressured up-push.
Sap is the syrup of the sense of self;
flower, its fountain finally made flesh.

Every hair in place erects
feeling for the insect God wishes
to flower on this flower,
pulsate, bumble, wade his knees
in golden powder till the slightest breeze
can knock him roaring nectared from his sling
dragging those softest saffron socks of rape.

The French comprehend.
How they eat, ravishing. How they drink,
breathing, licking, tasting. How they love,
braiding a third life in with work
and generation, *cinq à sept.*
How they betray, forsake, forget.

Flower Moon

It is always spring somewhere
in my empire.

— Pierre Cardin

Sometimes, rolling out light
like a bolt of lamé across the mounds
of fluid earth you command,
I see in you the tease, the pimp
the petulant mimic of the Haute Couture.

Do you know spring? You know the neaps
and floods. One day I see you
in an apple tree, a vast, pale blossom
freed and floating up
sheer as a scrap of voile. One night
prinked out with sprigs and twigs, all calico
strawberry fest and ribbons, up you come
over the village pony-rides, *O lente
lente currite noctis equi.*

Moon,
you are mad with fashion. Now brocade
wraps you in lustre like an empress; damask now
half whisper, melts and slips around your rounds.
All girl, you waltz among the seasick sway
of paper lights, snapping regatta flags,
the metronomic tilt of yellow masts,
while humping water suckles, fingers,
chortles under the pulsing floor.

Hot Moon

The past is a foreign country.
They do things differently there.

– L. P. Hartley

In ancient pre-Formican times
where marble soda fountains gleamed
in shafted light below the fans,
there where the cross-stitched Sampler men
sped like Egyptian couriers
on tiers and tiers of pyramid
all made of hand-dipped love and guilt
gift-boxed,
                incipience twanged
the wire rungs below the chairs
and mice with courage danced like motes
among the crumbs of sugar cones.
Our forelocks met and married over
one lime phosphate with two straws,
while the hot moon beyond the square
howled at the hounds her bitch disdain.
We heard her in the drug-like gloom.

The gold-fused bottles wink like gnomes
where deaths and aphrodisiacs
stand side by side. A mingled waft
orris root, ginger, lavender
enfolds us as in ambience.
Attars, tinctures, opiates –
each panacea has its pain –
promise some not-yet-earned surcease.
While turning leeches wax and wane
in wide-mouthed jars of weedy dark,
we hear the bugling moon again.

Buck and Wing: wooden toys

What toys we give our children teach
them theatre on the way to life.

− Erich Schwab

1.

One string through the crotch
dances the whole wooden clown.

2.

Harlequin's ruff, stiff
as Queen Elizabeth's,
holds up his baked, peaked
happy-cheeks, swallows the trembling
lower lip of his leer.
His gauze trunk, primitive
as the snake in Eden's box,
fights the little fingers
that depress its coils.
He's down. Now snap the latch.
He's up like a phallus
with a mind of its own.

3.

The chickens picking at the painted seed
in sequence on their paddle stage
bob like Matisse's dancers
while the ball-on-string below,
the God-machine, winds to its end
then withershins. Tireless
they peck at speckled illusion,
never hungry, never fed.

Never cock-ridden, never broody —
there is nothing to do but this, ever —
they bob their sequence, clattering.

Buck Moon

There is a buck in our wood, hunters say,
old beyond counting — no one has ever brought
him to a stumble. (Some think they grazed him.)
Old men in carpet slippers rock by the stove,
too old to go out, old as the buck perhaps,
and wait for their ruddy boys for news of his health
each night in hunting season.

                              But in safety's
season, walking out in the dark of the summer
moon, we sometimes hear him in the man-high grass
break for the forest as our voices' simmer
tangles the dancing field of fireflies.
Up from his loll like a feathered rocket
the mid-air measure of his wildness leaping
a long silence — an absent heart-beat —
he pounds; the second impact of his hoofs
shakes the whole floor of field between our toes.

Kicking the world away he ascends to grace:
there is this legend of this giant buck.

The Stag at Eve

At Noonan's Grille
the neon fails and wavers in the window
like a breath on frost, BOOTHS FOR LADIES.
There are no ladies. Here is a place
for men to conjugate, to decline: I age,
you (you familiar) age; he she it ages.
Or woman — of the woman (hers); to or for woman;
woman taken as object; vocative "Woman!";
by, from, with, in a woman. . .
Booths for ladies are empty at noon
at Noonan's, still I (a lady) am with you
always.   Rhyme thirst and lust,
rhyme first and last, rhyme dust
and worst. Such meanings are my business.

I know that your mouth hurts.
Your throat is a schoolroom corridor, plaster
and bile-green paint, wire-webbed at heat
and light intakes, wire at all the escapes;
to swallow is to choke chalk, to pulverize
and masticate the whole passage of childhood.
I am the water. I am what you drink.

Rhyme taste and must. Rhyme thrust and waste.
Rhyme lust and thirst. In a brown light
Noonan's dissolves the doddering afternoons.
The game is sepia in ale glow, in yellow smoke
twining in grey smoke, the game endlessly played;
men named like animals, the ardent cliché of dissolute
afternoons — the Tigers, the Rams, the Bruins —
tear flesh for the wet in it, slake
your heroic need.
                    Dazed or drowsing,
dismal hours are passed. The lilac sky
droops pendulous with promise over the river
where lights like frazzled flowers lurch
in dancelike pairs across the bridges, spill
thick, sinking honey-clots of gold in water.
They sink outcrying for continuations.

Dusk quickens life. Half prosperous, merely
weary work people stop at the bar for a splash
of wet on the risen gorge, and wend to homes
not bad nor half-bad. A blonde coiffe or wig,
a bumpsy-daisy gluteus-max, a silky thighflash
mix among, a little happiness and peace perhaps
for someone here as though from out of town.

You cringe, but crouch a little (may the road rise) —
you do identify, how good and tear-welling
all of it, all of it is. You try on your hands
like grey pallbearer's gloves, the feel of some hands
holding girl between them. But that's too near.
Snuggle your head in the softs of your palms
and pull at the amber, woman-warm milk of oblivion.
Surely in calm, in violet evening (swallow pride)
somewhere there's easement?

2.

Why, when I bless you, Irishman
May the road rise to meet you
why do you take me to mean
I hope you fall on your face?
May the road rise — well, it's all downhill
after Noonan's Grille. The lost populace
itinerates afloat on a swan lagoon of worse
and less diluted neutral spirit.

Night, from now on, mapped, is the fingerprint
of the city, a craziness divinely
patterned — each whorl a tale

of the seeming-aimless, brilliant longest
way home. If more rakish than most,
and more progressive, even your descent
is classical. It's a checkered career.
You are an alibi for God shot full of holes.
There are kettle-drums in your stapes.
They are deafening. Or hold the wall up,
guess at the menu, blind, blind. Somewhere
for hours — which hours? — you sleep straw-faced
on a straw car-seat, safe as a beast
in a barn. Some hours, when? in the velvet
tunnel of love of the movies, crawling fragments
of cartoon colours, moments of overwhelming
wide-screen, tight-pants thigh of aggressor come
toward, between a sleep and a sleep. . .

Now you are cheap and legion.
One more cerebellum wet and weighty as a car-
sponge; one more small, mild-mannered rumdum lost
among thousands, smote by the swollen moon.
Asleep in the drunk-tank. Asleep in the store-door.
Asleep in the box-car. Love, when night
is really still at last, I hear you
where you are. I hear your lip rub

at the rim for the last pull. Your throat —
my vagina — silt-choked amphorae
of the dreg-dark seas of need
identical we rock.

                    You pour and flood
with the sperm of burning booze
and, spawning glory, fall away like dead.

Sturgeon Moon

Pity her reach. I suspect she projects her bleeding
onto all of us. Her little monthly spell
of pseudocyesis — striated belly swollen,
the mien somehow brimmy, bland and shiny
with hope — time after time, all year
she weights us with incipient release.
Do we imagine needful cling in her fingers,
a tentacular feel to the touch of the light? Pity.

                                            But once,
listen — nobody's fool she — the pod elasticized
for this through all the tauten and slacken, bursting
expulses acres and acres of ears of corn.
Pearly as sweating butter, it grins in its sere lips
of husk. Death comes, says the sugared grin,
but first comes fructification. Sluiced like silage
in sorghum it comes — too much, too full
too wet too hot too sweet the gold red purple green
ferments of August tumble and pelt our amazed mouths
like bruises.

                     All night she spills imaginary young.
Dragonseed in paddies, troll-eggs in furry fens,
crysalid daemons on the under sides of flowers.
And in the vast and troublous sea, the mystic,
claret, suffocating, dumbstruck, desolate sea
welled up all-belly to accept her shattered light,
miles of seed sink to the dark forever.

Harvesting the Attic

1. *A Box of Death*

Opening attic boxes

The lungs begin to taste
of rodent's brine and urine.

My mother's dollies lie here
disassembled in mouse nests,
akimbo legs casual
as loving girls asleep
or raped ones murdered.
Bisque baby-faces stare
from holes. Fallen eye-pairs
roll back, look within.

All their elastics have let go.

2. Mouse Mother

She doesn't
so much choose
the stuff of the nest
as take whatever
will tear off,

Crepe paper, crochet-doily,
doll-sinew, book deckle,
satin wedding shoe.

Awful stuff, scratchy, hard
to get at, meagre.
But she does what she can
shredding and piling against
downbearing, desperate to have
the pool of heat fashioned
before she dumps her young.

3. Made Things

Here's the hula dancer I made.
Here's Santa Claus.
Here's May-baskets. Here's
new crepe paper, and a spool
thing that one runs it through to make
the rushes of the hula skirt.

Here are parts of linen pinwheels
Grandma made, sitting
in the bay window in the sun,
the sun on her shoulder,
and the heating pad to help
the sun, and the small hooded hook
darting from the fat pads of strictured
huge-jointed finger and thumb.
The hook flashes, winks sunbursts,
filigrees venomous pain.

4. Born Things

Her water rushes
from her like a freshet.
She hustles
into the nest, plumps
the walls up over.
Mother-warm, dark
as a tied pouch,
the nest receives them.
They cleat their mouths
to a thread of milk and begin
to put forth fine grey hairs.

5. Cakewalk

Come, Josephine:
Up the lazy river
in the gloaming
(you can bring Grace)
come to the church in the wildwood. . .

When bunnies hugged and bees had knees
and cats wore pyjamas, my parents were wed.
Her dress was made, every stitch,
by her mother, by hand. Ivory silk,
twenty fine tucks to the front (what
does a woman think about, sewing a dress
like that for an only daughter?) five
at each side of the silk-covered buttons.
Two insets of lace in the bodice, vertical,
three lace and two deep tucks in the skirt
going around. Lace insets also above
wide cuffs, and six small sleeve buttons
not for closure but trim.

(My father wore his uniform and puttees.
There was an arch of hard-rubbed swords.
I see it, although I am not really there.
I am born later, in the desert song.)

6. Paper Poem

I wonder how long it would take
to read through this attic.
Even to read the pictures
as I used to
on all these magazines.
Even just the Modern Priscillas.
Even just the sensual
flaming Luckies ads that made
my whole life less than expectation.

O leather Heloise and Abelard
with tissue leaves
with edges of true gilt

o true grit Rover Boys
intrepid Nancy Drew

o fairy book

o annals, Veritas,
Class of 1914

o Album with broken clasp
with slipping ovals
with sepia dead-people

old books O

7. Evictus

She ran,

an ooze of flowing
darkness running
all her young
at her paps latched on
like lurching schoolboys
hung on subway straps.

Harvest Moon

One would think that now of all times
(look at that title leaping off the page
like a cardboard moon on wires above
a soft-shoe song and dance)
I should be able to allow myself to let
a little doggerel out and bay a bit
about it, the heavenly cliché: Shine on!

Sail on!

       Well, I have lost the privilege
of doggerel. Through a leak in the pocket
where I kept fond hope like an amulet,
Bojangles ran out on me, too.
                  In age, in pain,
in despair, one is left with hard thought only —
bony, possibly vicious, altogether unwilling
to ring, rhyme, sing, chant, chime,
recant, reprise. I'd damn near sell
to any smoky fellow with a pointed pair
of ears for thirty jingles.

              What we harvest
we don't know — not when we sow. Seed
in the hand like old maid popcorn
box-bottoms; seed like pearls pouring off
a string; seed like the milk-weed floating;
seed, like Jack's bean in which there coils
a ladder to the moon — seed tells us
nothing.

       When did I plant this punishment,
this starveling's winter? Was the weather wrong?

The Hunted

When the dragons are gone
hunt unicorn.
(Artemis asked of Zeus,
at the age of three,
eternal virginity.)
Hunt all the unicorn *you* see.

When unicorn are gone
or less than visible
hunt gryphon: (bull
gryphon or cow
matters decreasingly now.)

Gryphon gone, hunt peacock,
bald eagle, snowy owl,
bison, egret, bear.

Horn

In misted green, gold-spangled
where the dawn, running, shakes the dew,
the curled horn pours molten pain
through the cur's ears, maddens
the smallish scent-scarred brain
to dream red runs in gulches
in the misted green.

Caged, then leashed, then loosed
in horn blare — that makes killers.
Horns also go to battle fields, to Hastings,
Agincourt. Horns also issue heralds, fanfare
strangers, poisoners, bridegrooms, gods on swans.
The cornua yield the globuled pageantry:
the cup below inclines to take the blood.

In mist, in green, horns ring the burnished air
clangorous as the dog torn from his cry
his gullet strewn in ribbons around his throes.

Hunter's Moon

1.

They come on paws like lesser stars,
on twinkle-toes across the wars
of beast and god, and man and beast
and God and man, the mythic pair —
Ursa Major and Baby Bear —
and turn like captive bears on chain
around, around their pole again.

2.

Artemis, the moon lady, the white goddess, the
professional virgin, the so-called 'queen and hunt-
ress chaste and fair', left us the legend of the
stellar bears:
Her friends were sworn to be as chaste as she
herself. All her nymphs. But Zeus seduced one
anyway. Jealous Artemis changed it to bear, Zeus's
new seed was born the Little Bear, and Artemis
set her frustrate pack to hunt them down. Zeus
snatched and hid them in the sky. But short-
leashed, haunted, sleepless, they pad around the
polar star and never dip below the warm horizon's
furry edge.

3.

(Yet some in vicious
myth and rhyme
say it was Artemis
that time
herself, and better
girls than she
lay down and parted
knee from knee
for Zeus, if
no more willingly. . .)

4.

   To escape him, or elude, other authorities say,
she applied white-face, river-gypsum; moreover she
turned *herself* into the bear. Whited sepulchre,
painted lady, grizzly, it was all one, all Artemis
to Zeus, from whom, as from God always, I do
believe there is no hiding.

Beaver Moon

A girl turned into a tree, in a legend.
In several legends. I have a tree
that turned into a boy. First there was the boy,
that is, taking the light in one particular field
and laying it this way, that way, his tractor
deft as a Chinese brush — as delicate and true -
laying the windrows back in a sheer gold wash.

He disappeared, Ezra, pouff, in the back seat
of a taxicab on Cambridge Street. In the very act
of refusing the first not-aspirin pill he ever saw
he entered the beady eye of speed and terror.
In the tunnels, screams resonate. All the first
summer he was gone, and all the second, the tree,
the aspen, became Ezra. The storms came
and bent it double, dragged his hair on the ground.
The tree hardened bent, like a stooped adolescent,
but never snapped, nor lost the inner music
nor the way with light.

                    When he came home
who was he? Something scuttled and peeked out
from time to time, small as a pellet
in a sleighbell. Was that his vestige?

Beaver moon, I dub you Aspen moon
in the old fashion, tapping you thrice on the shoulder,
laughing at title, laughing at ceremonial, I,
and I and Ezra as always laughing together.

The beaver builds his house of aspen,
sucks and gnaws his winter life from aspen.
Ezra and Jean here name his moonlight aspen.

Pathetic Fallacy

The Indians call the beaver
"Little Man of the Woods."
Marvel at his handwork,
how he diverts, divides,
builds and retains his watery
acre, marvel how he domes
and clays the high, dry house,
marvel how he lives therein
sober, monogamous!

Safety is all. Shore the dam.
Mend the noise in the wall.

Cold Moon

The cold moon looks alike on the black city
iron escarpments, rat holes, coals and klinkers
(Liverpool, Kiel, New York) and on rose-red
Petra, or Boston's blush on the yellow Charles.
On golden cities, Petersburg, Rome, New Orleans,
and on white cities — the marble, the sugar cities —
Odessa, and San Francisco, and Budapest.

White light through tinkling air. This coldest moon
beams nothing down that's earned, dreamed or reflected.
But the white city, loving, beams love back.

The White City

Our fantasy, how much of it is
banished memory? How much of that
is vanished history?
       — *Les Illuminations Byzances
de St. Dommage, 1390*

and ran with you
took your hand and ran
until we fell
never looked back

The Old One, the dark cards
sweet with his hands' oils —
with magic garlic, flowers
of rosemary leaf, white-green
and gold-green grapes —
he read it, spun the *rota*
how many separate times?
Shuffle the leaves from the wands.
Shake off the stars from the coins.
Cut to the right, the left.
The cards keep falling the same.
Hurl them — wouldn't they land
in the Byzantine cross?
My sky-clean, cup-brimming
lady covered and crossed
pressed up, pressed forth
crowned, drawn by the sure
same meanings, powers
moving us now? The ladder

ascending still to the seven
of wands, to the hill boy,
his staff fronting enemies
rooted and growing?
(Courage in adversity.)

came to rest
in the elbow of the river
sundrenched in the saffron light
of Suleiman's pilaf-bowl
lay sheltered like a flower
in the hammock of hand
lay held and holding
kernel in husk you held me
safe from the mountains' wind
rested and slept

Time wags its metal tail. The pitch-pipe
gentles, orients, black flocks of notes.
Do not all music lessons end this way? How
not succumb and run away with the fiddler?
The bow will detonate avowel in the string —
an act of love. And lady, thus you leave
master and sons, repasts and rows of shoon,
led by widening water rings in your ears.

and had or didn't have
hard goods
vases and bowls
pictures and books
or money-things   feasts
gardens   southern travels

had or didn't have
sometimes places   trysts
at the column
at the cherub clock

sometimes riven
like the double city
a featherstitch of seven
bridges pulled askew
hands yanked apart
gaze interrupted
by a giant wheel
with spokes of blindness
all people passing
turned to enemies
interpositions

sometimes ran again
goose-glad to have
a fish on a spit
a hatful of blackberries
somehow music
music was playing
somewhere the whole time

Time and again I erase, omit
or forget the end. Call you friend.
But light around your head.
But the thickening cage
of withies. The dark. The wind.
But pretend that not this time
and somewhere else, and all things
being otherwise. . .

Not here. Not us. Not now.
And now, here, us.